THE MORALS
of
ECONOMIC
INTERNATIONALISM

WITH AN EXCERPT FROM
Imperialism,
The Highest Stage Of Capitalism
BY V. I. LENIN

By

J. A. HOBSON

First published in 1920

British Library Cataloguing-in-Publication Data
A catalogue record for this book is available
from the British Library

CONTENTS

———————

THE HIGHEST
STAGE OF CAPITALISM

AN EXCERPT FROM
Imperialism,
The Highest Stage Of Capitalism
BY V. I. LENIN

During the past fifteen or twenty years, especially after the Spanish-American War (1898) and the Anglo-Boer War (1899-1902), the economic and also the political literature of the old and new world has more and more often adopted the term "imperialism" in order to characterise the epoch in which we live. In 1902, *Imperialism*, a work by English economist, J. A. Hobson, was published in London and New York. The author, who adopts the point of view of bourgeois social reformism and pacifism, which in essence is identical with the present position of the ex-Marxist, K. Kautsky, gives a very good and detailed description of the principal economic and political characteristics of imperialism.... Hobson, in his work on imperialism, marks the years 1884-1900 as being the period of intensified "expansion" of the chief European states. According to his estimate, England during these years acquired 3.7 million square miles of territory with a population of 57 million ; France acquired 3.6 million ; Germany one million square miles with 16.7 million inhabitants ; Belgium 900,000 square miles with 30 million inhabitants ; Portugal 800,000 square miles with 9 million inhabitants. The quest for colonies by all capitalist states at the end of the nineteenth century, and particularly since the 1880's, is a well-known fact in the history of diplomacy and of foreign policy.

THE MORALS
OF
ECONOMIC
INTERNATIONALISM

IT ought not to be the case that there is one standard of morality for individuals in their relations with one another, a different and a slighter standard for corporations, and a third and still slighter standard for nations. For, after all, what are corporations but groupings of individuals for ends which in the last resort are personal ends? And what are nations but wider, closer, and more lasting unions of persons for the attainment of the end they have in common, i.e., the commonwealth. Yet we are well aware that the accepted and operative standards of morality differ widely in the three spheres of conduct. If a soul is imputed at all to a corporation, it is a leather soul, not easily penetrable to the probings of pity or compunction, and emitting much less of the milk of human kindness than do the separate souls of its directors and stockholders in their ordinary human relations. There is a sharp recognition of this inferior moral make-up of a corporation in the attitude of ordinary men and women, who, scrupulously honest in their dealings with one another, slide almost unconsciously to an altogether lower level in dealing with a railroad or insurance company. This attitude is due, no doubt, partly to a resentment of the oppressive power which great corporations are believed to exercise, evoking a desire "to get a bit of your own back"; partly to a feeling that any slight injury to, or even fraud perpetrated on, a corporation will be so distributed as to inflict no appreciable harm on any individual stockholder. But largely it is the result of a failure to envisage a corporation as

9

a moral being at all, to whom one owes obligations. Corporations are in a sense moral monsters; we say they behave as such and we are disposed to treat them as such.

The standard of international morality, particularly in matters of commercial intercourse, is on a still lower level. If, indeed, one were to press the theoretic issue, whether a state or a nation is a morally independent being, or whether it is in some sense or degree a member of what may be called an incipient society of states or nations, nearly every one would sustain the latter view. We should be reminded that there was such a thing as international law, however imperfect its sanctions might be, and that treaties, alliances, and other agreements between nations implied the recognition of some moral obligation. How weak this interstate morality is appears not merely from the fact that under strong temptation governments repudiate their most express and solemn agreements—to that temptation individuals sometimes yield in their dealings with one another—but also from the nature of the defence which they make of such repudiation. The plea of state necessity, which Germany made for the violation of the neutrality of Belgium, and which was stretched to cover the brutal mishandling of the Belgian people, is unfortunately but an extreme instance of conduct to which every state has had recourse at times, and—still more significant—which every state defends by adducing the same maxim, "*salus reipublicæ suprema lex*".

Here is the sharpest distinction between individual and national morality. There are certain deeds which a good and honorable man would not do even to save his life; there are no deeds, which it is admitted that a statesman, acting on behalf of his country, may not do to save that country. It is foolish to try to shirk this disconcerting admission. The Machiavellian doctrine of "reason of state" is, in the last resort, the accepted standard of national conduct. This does not signify that a nation and its government admit no obligation to fulfil their promises, or even voluntarily to perform good offices for other nations, but that there is always implied the reservation that the necessity, or, shall we say, the vital interests, of the nation override, cancel, and nullify all such obligations. And when "necessity" is stretched to cover any vital interest or urgent need, it is easy to recognize on what a slippery slope such international morality reposes.

International morality is impaired, however, not only by this feeble sense of mutual obligation, but by the still more injurious assumption of conflicting interests between nations. Nations are represented not merely as self-centered, independent moral systems, but as, in some degree, mutually repellent systems. This notion is partly the product of the false patriotic teaching of our schools and press, which seek to feed our sense of national unity more upon exclusive than inclusive sentiments. Nations are represented as rivals and competitors in some struggle for power, or greatness, or prestige, instead of as coöperators in the general advance of civilization. This presumption of opposing interests is, of course, more strongly marked in the presentation of commercial relations than in any other. Putting the issue roughly, but with substantial truth, the generally accepted image of international trade is one in which a number of trading communities, as, for instance, the United States, Britain, Germany, France, Japan, etc., are engaged in striving, each to win for itself, and at the expense of the others, the largest possible share of a strictly limited objective—the world market.

Now there are three fatal flaws in this image. First comes the false presentation of the United States, Britain, Germany, and other political beings in the capacity of trading firms. So far as world or international trade is rightly presented as a competitive process, that competition takes place, not between America, Britain, Germany, but between a number of separate American, British, German firms. The immediate interests of these firms are not directed along political lines. Generally speaking, the closer rivalry is between firms belonging to the same nation and conducting their business upon closely similar conditions. One Lancashire cotton exporter competes much more closely with other Lancashire exporters than he does with German, American, or Japanese exporters of similar goods. So it is everywhere, save in the exceptional times and circumstances in which governments themselves take over the regulation and conduct of foreign trade.

For certain purposes it is, no doubt, convenient to have balances and analyses of foreign trade presented separately, so as to show the volumes and values of different goods which pass from the members of one nation to those of another. But the imputation of political significance to these statistics, taken either in aggregate or in relation to separate countries, as if they were themselves indices of public gain or public loss, has most injurious reactions upon the intelligent understanding of commerce.

The second flaw is the assumption of a limited amount of market, which carries with it the assumption that the groups of traders, gathered under their national flags, are engaged in a conflict in which they are entitled to embroil their governments. By tariff bargaining and by all sorts of diplomatic weapons each government is called upon to assist its nationals and to cripple or exclude the nationals of other states. Now it is untrue that the world market is strictly limited, with the consequence that every advance of one group of traders is at the expense of another group. The world market is indefinitely expansible, and is always expanding; and commercial experience shows that the rapid expansion of the overseas trade of one country does not preclude the expansion of trade of other countries. I do not, of course, deny that at a particular time and in relation to some particular lucrative opportunity, genuine clashes of interests may arise. But, envisaging the whole range of foreign commerce, one feels that the image of it as a prize which governments can, and ought to win for their traders at the expense of the traders supported by other governments, has been a most fertile source of international misunderstanding.

Perhaps the worst of the three fallacies, and in a sense

the deepest-rooted, is the concept of export trade as of more value than import trade. This is often traced back to the time when governments deemed it desirable to accumulate in their countries treasures of gold and silver and to this end encouraged the sale of goods abroad and discouraged the payment for them in foreign goods. There are, however, modern supporters of the assumption that it is more important to sell than to buy, although the money received for sales has no other significance or value than its power to buy, and trade can only be imaged truly as an exchange of goods for goods in which the processes of selling and of buying are complementary.

The economic explanation of the double falsehood of dividing buying from selling and of imputing a higher value to the latter process, lies beyond the scope of this address. But the injuries resulting from the superior pressure upon governments of organized bodies of producers and merchants who have things to sell, to the detriment of the consuming public who have only buying needs, are too grave matters to be neglected here. It is not too much to say that, if the interests of consumers and the interests of producers weighed equally in the eyes of governments, as they should, the strongest of all obstacles to a peaceful, harmonious society of nations would be overcome. For the suspicions, jealousies, and hostilities of nations are inspired more by the tendency of groups of producers to misrepresent their private interests as the good of their respective countries than by any other single circumstance.

This analysis has seemed necessary in order to clear away the intellectual and moral fogs which prevent a true realization of the economic, and therefore the moral, interdependence of nations. For every bond of economic interest involves moral obligation also. If it is true that the fabric of commercial relations is all the time being knit closer between the different peoples of the earth, then the moral isolation and the antagonism which earlier statecraft inculcated, and which still obsess so many minds, must be dissipated and give place to active sentiments of human coöperation.

There were, indeed, those who thought that already the web of commerce and finance had been woven strong enough to save nations from the calamity of war. Their miscalculation arose from underestimating the power over the mind and the passions of that false image of trade. But because the modern internationalism of commerce and finance did not prove strong enough to stem the full and sudden tide of war passions fed from the barbarous traditions of a dateless past, we ought not to disparage the potentiality of this internationalism as the foundation of a new and better world order. For, though those bonds of common interest broke under the strain of war, the confusion in which we find ourselves without them is itself a terrible testimony to their value. The enforced sundering of ordinary trade relations between members of different countries has taught two clear lessons. The first is this: that hardly any civilized nation is or can be economically independent in respect to essential supplies or industries. There is no European country that does not rely for the subsistence of its inhabitants upon supplies of goods and raw materials from foreign lands, mostly from countries outside the European continent. While Britain both leaned more heavily upon other countries and contributed most to other countries from her surplus produce, every other country, in larger or less degree—great countries such as France, Germany, Austria, Italy, little ones like Belgium, Holland, Switzerland, Scandinavia, and Denmark—were increasingly dependent upon outside sources for their livelihood. It is true that there remained a very few great backward countries, such as Russia and China, where a life of economic isolation was possible had they been willing to dispense with the higher products of civilized industry and with the fertilizing streams of capital without which progress is impossible. No civilized European country was self-sufficing in the vital factors of a productive and progressive civilization—food, raw materials, machinery, fuel, transport, finance, and adequate supplies of skilled labor. The services which countries near or distant rendered to one another were becoming constantly more numerous, more complex, and more urgent. The obstructions and stoppages of war has driven home the lesson painfully to the inhabitants of every European country, belligerent or neutral. What lesson? That we have erred in permitting ourselves to grow dependent on the industry, goodwill, and intercourse of other nations, and that we should endeavor to hark back to an earlier economic state of national independence? Well, there are even in Britain rhetorical politicians who speak of the necessity of retaining all "key" or "essential" industries within their national control—who propose to reverse the tide of social evolution by some flimsy apparatus of tariffs and subsidies. This is impossible. The war has left the European peoples, one and all, more than ever dependent for their economic livelihood upon one another, and upon the material resources and labor of other continents.

The second lesson is that, other things equal, it is the most highly civilized and highly developed countries that are the most dependent upon others. In a word, there is a presumption that economic internationalism is an essential feature of civilization.

You will observe that so far I have made no mention of America. And yet all that I have been saying is, in a sense, introductory to the unique problem presented by this country. America is the only civilized country in the world that is virtually self-sufficing as regards the primary requirements of her economic life. Her soil can and does supply nearly all her essential foods, her natural resources include the materials of her great textile, metal, and other basic industries, the heat, light, electricity, and other forms of natural energy which satisfy her national needs. She has access to skilled and unskilled labor sufficient to develop and utilize all these natural resources. Most of her pre-war imports might be placed under four heads: articles of luxury and taste in dress, jewelry, etc.; certain chemical and other scientific products; supplementary supplies of some foods and materials, from other countries of the American continent, for manufactures and export trade; and a number of tropical products, almost all of subsidiary significance in the production and consumption of the American people. This slight dependence upon foreign countries has been considerably reduced as the result of war exigency. The art products of France and Italy, the fine textile goods from Britain, the dye-stuffs, drugs, and scientific instruments from Germany—in a word, the great bulk of the imports from Europe, have either been cut out of American consumption or have been displaced, temporarily, at any rate, by home products. For several generations the main dependence of America upon Europe and particularly upon Britain was for capital to supplement home savings that she might make use of the stream of immigrant labor in the development of her great continent. This dependence upon European capital, of greatly diminishing importance during the last three decades has, of course, now been reversed, and the principal European countries are heavy debtors to the United States.

One other important economic lesson war experience has taught, viz., the vast capacity for increased productivity which every industrial nation possesses, and America especially, in better organization and fuller utilization of natural and human resources. It is evident that, far from the age of great inventions and of mechanical development drawing to a close, we are in the actual process of reaching new discoveries in wealth production, which will make the most famous advances of the nineteenth century mean by comparison. But without drawing upon a speculative future, a better and more systematic application of the knowledge which has been already tested—enlarged production, elimination of waste, and improved business methods—is clearly capable of doubling or trebling the output of material wealth without involving any excessive strain upon human effort.

Here, as in other ways, America stands in a place of unique vantage by reason of the magnitude and variety of her national resources, and the vigor and enterprise of her people.

It is evident that, if any country can afford to stand alone in full economic self-sufficiency, that country is America. It is feasible for America to contract within very narrow limits her commercial and political relations with the rest of the world, or, if she chooses, to confine her commercial and financial relations to this continent, leaving the old world to get on by itself as well as it can. This view is, indeed, conformable with the main tradition of American history up to the close of the last century. Even the Spanish war, with its sequel of imperialism, was but a slight and reparable breach in this tradition. The world war seems at first sight to have plunged America deeper into the European trough. But even this more serious committal is not irretrievable. She can step back to the doctrine and policy of 'America for Americans' and refuse any organic contact with a troublesome, a quarrelsome and, as it seems, a ruined Europe. America's economic status in Europe is not such as to preclude her taking this course. I may be reminded that the indebtedness of Europe to America is a solid economic bond, for it cannot be presumed that America would pursue the policy of liberalism so far as to cancel this debt. But, large as is this credit, it need not constitute a strong or a lasting bond of commerce, compelling America to receive such large imports of goods from Europe as materially to impair her self-sufficiency. A large and increasing part of the interest and capital of this indebtedness would be defrayed by the expenditure of American travellers and residents in Europe, while the importation of objects of art and luxury would not interfere appreciably with the policy of economic nationalism. If America decides to go no further in this business, it will not be too late to draw out.

The choice before her is momentous. So far I have presented it as an economic problem. It is also quite evidently a political and moral problem of the first significance, for economic national self-sufficiency is a phase of political independence. But business and politics alike belong to the wider art of human conduct; and the choice before America is primarily a moral choice.

By saying this I do not wish to appear to prejudge the issue. I have always felt that a stronger case could be made for the political and economic isolation of America than for that of any other country, partly because, as I have said, she has within her political domain all the resources of national well-being; partly, also, because it is of supreme importance that the great experiment of democracy should not be unduly hampered by excessive inpourings of ill-assimilable foreign blood, and by dangerous contacts with obsolete or inapplicable European institutions. As an economist, steeped in the principles of Cobden and his British school of liberals, my predilections (prejudices if you will) have always been in favor of the freest possible movement, alike of trade and persons, and against fiscal protection and immigrant restrictions. But, when confronted with the special situation of America, I have recognized that a reasoned argument could be addressed to prove that the economy of national security and progress for this country lay along the lines of political, economic and defensive self-containedness. I am convinced that many must be led to support this policy, not on grounds of selfishness, because they desire to conserve for America alone her great opportunities, and not mainly from fear, lest America should be embroiled again in the dangerous quarrels of distant European nations, but because they are animated by that pure desire, which has inspired so many generations of high-minded Americans, that American democracy should grow to its full stature by its own unaided efforts and save the world by its example.

I wish to give due respect to the sincerity of this conviction the more because I wish to lay before you some grounds for questioning its ultimate validity. It is no problem of abstract politics or ethics with which I here confront your minds, but one of concrete and immediate urgency. Distinctively economic in its substance, it brings right into the daylight the hitherto obscure issue of the duty of nations as members of an actual or potential society of nations. As a result of the destruction of war a large part of Europe lies today in economic ruin. By that I do not only, or chiefly, refer to the material havoc wrought by the direct operations of war in France, Belgium, Poland, Servia, and elsewhere. I mean the imminent starvation which this winter awaits large populations of those and other countries, both our allies and our late enemies, and the misery and anarchy arising from their utter inability to resume the ordinary processes of productive industry. It is not only food and clothing but raw materials, tools, machinery, transport, and fuel that are lacking over a large part of the European continent. If they are left to their own unaided resources, millions of these people, especially in Russia, Poland, Austria, and sections of the late Turkish Empire, will perish. They cannot feed themselves. The land remains, but large tracts of it have been untilled; large numbers of the peasantry have fallen in the war, or are wandering as disbanded soldiers, far from home; the women and the aged and the children, underfed and broken in health and spirit, are utterly unequal to the task of growing the food for their livelihood. The factories and workshops are idle or are ill-equipped, for materials, tools, and fuel are everywhere lacking; unemployment holds large industrial populations in destitution and despair. Even where plant and materials are present, the physical strength of the workers is so let down that efficient productivity is impossible. Even in countries that are not war-broken, the blockade, and the long stoppage of normal commerce, have caused great scarcity of many important foods and materials, and famine prices bring grievous suffering to the poorer classes. Britain alone among the belligerent countries is not in immediate distress, but only because she has had larger outside resources and larger borrowing powers on which to draw. Even the few neutral nations which are said to have profited by war are severely crippled by the lack of some essentials of their economic life.

All in different degrees are economic victims of the havoc and the waste of war. It is not Central Europe only, together with large parts of the Balkans, of Russia, and of Eastern Asia, that is in this evil plight. Europe as a whole is unprovided with the foodstuffs with which to feed its population and the raw materials with which to furnish employment. If there were prevailing among them the best of wills and of coöperative arrangements, the European peoples could not keep themselves alive this winter and make any substantial advance towards reparation of the damage of war and industrial recovery. If human coöperation is to save these weak and desperate peoples, it must be a coöperation of more than the nations of Europe. Only by the better provided nations of the world coming to the rescue can the worse-provided nations survive and recover. It would be foolish to mince words in so grave an issue. We are all acquainted with the main facts of the world situation and are familiar with the place which America occupies in it as the chief repository of those surpluses of foods, materials, and manufactured goods which Europe needs so sorely. The term 'surplus' is, of course, somewhat deceptive. Surplus depends largely on home consumption, itself an elastic condition. But for practical purposes we may take the exportable surplus to mean the product which remains for sale abroad after the normal wants of the home population are supplied. It might mean something more, viz., that the home population would voluntarily keep down or reduce their consumption, in order that more might be available for export. The American people actually did exercise this self-denying ordinance to an appreciable extent, in order to help win the war. Are they willing to do the same in order to help the world in a distress as dire as war itself?

It may be said, perhaps truly, that this presumes that America is in the peace as much as she was in the war, that she has decided to link her destiny closely and lastingly with that of Europe, that she definitely accepts a proffered place as a member of the society of nations, and under circumstances which make an immediate call upon her economic and financial resources in a manner in which there can be no direct reciprocity.

Now it may reasonably be urged that America is not prepared for such a committal, that such obligations as she undertook, as an associated power, in the conduct of the war, terminate with the making of peace; and that, as regards the future structure of international relations, she proposes to preserve full freedom to coöperate with other nations, or to stand alone, according to her estimate of each occasion.

It is here convenient to treat separately two issues which are none the less closely related, viz., the issue of international coöperation for the immediate work of the salvage and restoration of Europe, and the issue of a permanent coöperation or agreement for the equitable use of the economic resources of the world. The urgency for Europe of the first issue has been already indicated. If the weaker European nations are left to the ordinary play of economic laws for the supplies they need, they must lapse into starvation and social anarchy. A lifting of the war blockades and embargoes hardly helps them. The formal restoration of free commerce is little better than a mockery to those who lack the power to buy and sell. Free commerce would simply mean that America's surplus, the food, materials, and manufactured goods she has to sell abroad, would be purchased exclusively by those more prosperous foreigners who have the means to pay in money, or in export goods available for credit purposes. Now the populations and the governments of these broken countries have neither money nor goods in hand. The return of peace has left them with depleted purses and empty stores. If the purchase and consumption of the available surplus of foods, materials, and manufactures from America and other prosperous countries is distributed according to the separate powers of purchase in the European countries, the countries and the classes of population which are least in need will get all, those which are most in need, nothing. How can it be otherwise, if immediate ability to pay is the criterion? In ordinary times the machinery of international finance does tend to distribute surplus stocks according to the needs of the different nations, for the production of the actual goods for export trade with which imports are paid for, the true base of credit, is continually proceeding. But the war broke this machinery of regular exchange. It cannot be immediately restored. America or Argentina cannot sell their surplus wheat in the ordinary way to Poland, Austria, Belgium and other needy countries, because, largely for the very lack of these goods and materials, their industries are not operating, so that the goods they should produce, upon which credit would be built, are not forthcoming.

This is one of the most terrible of the vicious circles in which the war has bound the world. The weak nations cannot buy, because they are not producing goods to sell; they cannot produce, because they cannot buy. What are the strong nations, those with surplus goods, the transport, and the credit, going to do about it? It is a question of emergency finance based on an emergency morality. The nations which have surpluses to sell abroad must not only send the goods but provide the credit to pay for them if they are to reach the peoples that need them most. But how, it is said, can you expect the business man in America or any other country to perform such an act of charity? How can you expect them to sell to those who have not credit and cannot pay, instead of selling to those who have credit and can pay? The answer is sometimes stated thus. It is not charity you are asked to perform, but such consideration for customers as a really intelligent sense of self-interest will endorse. We ask you to put up a temporary bridge over the financial chasm in order to afford time for this restoration of the ordinary processes of exchange. If the enfeebled industrial peoples can be furnished now with foods and materials they will set to work, and in the course of time they will be able, out of the product of their industry, to repay your advances and reestablish the normal circle of exchange.

In presenting this course as a policy of intelligent self-interest, I am not really disparaging the claims of humanity or of morals. I am merely maintaining the utilitarian ethics which insist that morality, the performance of human obligations, is the best policy, that policy which in the long run will yield the fullest satisfaction to social beings. If I were an American exporter in control of large amounts of food, it would doubtless pay me better personally at the present time to sell it to firms in European countries which have good credit, for consumption by people who are in no great want. As an individual business man, I could hardly do otherwise with any assurance of financial profit. I am not here presenting the issue as a matter of individual morals. If the surplus of economic supplies is to be distributed according to needs, on an emergency credit basis adjusted to that end, it is evident that this can be done only by international coöperation. This shifts the moral problem from the individual to the nation. Rich nations, or their governments, are asked to assist poor nations by making an apportionment of goods and credit which the individual members of the rich nations, the owners of the surplus, would not make upon their own account. The edge of this issue should not be blunted. If the people and government of America were only concerned to let their individual citizens extort the highest prices they could get for their surplus in the best markets, they would let Central and Eastern Europe starve. If, however, they also take into account the social, political, and economic reactions of a starving Europe upon the future of a world in which they will have to live as members of a world society which must grow ever closer in its physical, economic, and spiritual contacts, they may decide differently. The issue arises in the highest economic sphere, that of finance. Are the nations and governments of the world sufficiently alive to the urgency of the situation to enter into an organization of credit for the emergency use of transport and for the distribution of foods and materials on a basis of proved needs? The richer nations, in proportion to their resources, would appear to be called upon to make a present sacrifice for the benefit of the poorer nations in any such pooling of credit facilities. That risk of sacrifice, however, need not be great, and need not be felt at all by the individual members of rich nations, provided that the hitherto unused resources of national credit can be built into a strong structure of mutual support. If America were invited to find adequate credits for Italian or Polish needs at the present time, she might well hesitate. But if a consortium of European governments, including Britain and the richer neutrals, were joint guarantors of such advances, this coöperative basis might furnish the necessary confidence. It is not within my scope to discuss the various forms a financial consortium might take; whether America, as representative of the creditor nations, should enter such a consortium, or should approach the organized credit of Europe in the capacity of a friendly uncle. It must suffice here to indicate the moral test which this grave issue presents to the nations regarded as economic powers.

Upon the policy adopted for this emergency will doubtless depend in large measure the whole future of economic internationalism. For not only does confidence grow with effective coöperation, but upon this post-war coöperation between nations for an emergency commerce and finance, or its rejection, will depend not only America's future place in a world society but the structure of that world society in its essential character.

For in each great nation of the world the same great choice, the same great struggle of contending principles and policies, is taking place. National self-dependence or internationalism—that is everywhere the issue. It is true that in no European country can that issue be so sharply presented as in America. For economic self-sufficiency in a full sense and, therefore, political isolation, is not possible for any European state. Even a peaceful and reviving Russia must lean upon her more advanced neighbors for the economic essentials of capital and organizing skill. But the several nations can strive to reduce their interdependence and their national aid to the narrowest dimensions, and where they cannot free themselves from extraneous alliances they can restrict the area of economic dependence within a chosen circle. Britain, for example, could set her policy closely and consistently to make her world-wide empire into a self-sufficing system, and if, as is likely, she learned that even the diversified fifth of the entire globe which owns allegiance to her Crown could not satisfy all her wants, she could eke out this inadequacy with some carefully selected and purchased friendships.

This harking back to an economic nationalism is a natural reaction of the war, and is fed by a dangerous and precarious peace. Fear, greed, and suspicion prompt the victorious nations to guard their gains by reverting to a close nationalism or a ringed alliance; humiliation, without humility, the bitter pain of thwarted ambitions, resentment at their punishment, dispose the vanquished nations to keep their own company and form if possible, an economic system of their own. A prolonged war, followed by a bad peace, may leave this indelible scar upon the growing economic internationalism of the world.

The richly nourished patriotism of war breeds divisions and antagonisms which are easily exploited afterwards by political, racial, religious, and cultural passions, but most of all by economic interests.

Before the war internationalism was visibly advancing with every fresh decade. The bonds of commercial and financial intercourse between the peoples of different countries were continually woven closer; the policy of self-sufficiency was continually giving way before the superior economy of specialization on a basis of natural or acquired advantages. Any reversal of this policy would be far costlier than may at present appear, even for those countries best qualified by size and resources to stand alone.

For it is not merely the direct sacrifice of the wider world economy of production and exchange, the advantage of a wider over a narrower area of free commerce, that is involved. It is the indirect perils and costs of the policy of close nationalism or restricted economic alliances that count heaviest. For economic nationalism means protective and discriminative tariffs, and a conservation of national, imperial or allied resources within a circle of favored beneficiaries. This is the temptation held out to the British people today by the protectionist interests working upon the animosity of the war spirit and the sentiment of imperialism. The welding of an empire into an independent economic system, the conservation of essential or key industries and the safeguarding of our industries against "dumping," are the ostensible objectives of a policy whose chief driving motive and end is the establishment of strong industrial, commercial and financial trusts and combinations, defended by tariff walls, and endowed with the profits of monopoly.

There are two difficulties in such a course of action, which, though especially urgent in the case of Britain, beset every great country that chooses the same path, and not least, America. The first is the fomentation of a class war, based upon divisions of interests between capital and labor, producer and consumer, protected and unprotected industries. The initial skirmishes of such a conflict are already visible in every country where wages, prices, and profiteering are burning issues. I would most earnestly appeal to thoughtful citizens in this as in my own country to pause before heaping fuel on these fires. For the policy of national self-sufficiency or isolation means nothing less than this. Not merely does it strengthen the power of capitalistic combinations and thereby incite labor unions to direct action, blackmailing demands, and sabotage. Not merely does it let loose upon the business world all sorts of ill-considered governmental interferences for the fixation of prices or subsidies to consumers. It keeps alive and feeds the habit and the spirit of strife. For it was no accident that the great international war left as its legacy smaller international class wars in European countries. Remove from a nation the economic supports it formerly received from other nations, markets wherein to buy and sell, and you starve that nation; and starvation breeds class war and anarchy. Can any one doubt this with the terrible examples of Russia and Hungary before their eyes? But it is not a matter of war conditions alone. Carry through a policy of economic nationalism, under which all the large and well-equipped nations and empires conserve for their exclusive uses the national resources they command, and what

26

happens? The smaller and the poorer nations, however free in the political sense, become their economic bond slaves, at the mercy of the master states for their foods and other necessaries of life. Take the case of Austria under the new conditions, with a thick population concentrated in a great political capital suddenly deprived of all free access to its former sources of supply and the markets it used to serve. For her it is a sentence of economic strangulation. Here is an extreme instance of the effect of economic isolation on a weak country. But the dangerous truth may be more broadly stated. A very few great empires and nations today control the whole available supplies of many of the foods, fabrics, and metals, the shipping and finance, that are essential to the livelihood and progress of every civilized people. Are Britain, America, France, and Japan—and especially the two greatest of these powers—going to absorb or monopolize for their exclusive purposes of trade or consumption these supplies which every country needs, or are they going to let the rest of the world have fair access to them? I think this to be upon the whole the most important of the many urgent issues that confront us. For, if close nationalism or imperialism should prevail, the weaker placed nations could not acquiesce. Close economic nationalism is not for them a possibility. They must win access to the world's supplies, peacefully if possible, or else by force.

The fatality of the great choice is thus evident. Nations must and will fight for the means of life. Close economic nationalism or imperialism on the part of the great empires must, therefore, compel the restricted countries to organize force for their economic liberation. This in turn will compel the great empires to maintain strong military and naval defences. It is impossible for the other nations of the earth to leave the essential supplies of metals, foods, and oils, and the control of transport in the exclusive possession of one or a few close national corporations or a permanent "Big Four." Under such conditions the sacrifices of the great war would have been made in vain. Nothing would have been done to end war, or to rescue the world from the burden of militarism. The pre-war policy of contending alliances and of competing armaments, draining more deeply than ever the surplus incomes of each people, would be resumed. And it would bring no sense of security, but only the postponement of further inevitable conflicts in which the very roots of western civilization might perish.

The renewed and intolerable burdens of such a militarism, with its accompaniments of autocracy, must let loose class war in every nation which has gone through the agony of the European struggle and has seen the great hope of a peaceful internationalism blighted.

It is predominantly upon America and Britain that this great moral economic choice rests, the choice on which the safety and the progress of humanity depend. A refusal by either of these great powers can make any league of nations and any economic internationalism impossible. The confident consent of both can furnish the material and moral support for the new order. If these countries in close concerted action were prepared to place at the service of the new world order their exclusive or superior resources of foods, materials, transport and finance— the economic pillars of civilization—the stronger pooling their resources with the weaker for the rescue work in this dire emergency, this political coöperation would supply that mutual confidence and goodwill without which no governmental machinery of a League of Nations, however skilfully contrived, can begin to work.

I have spoken of Britain and America as the two countries upon whose choice this supreme issue hangs. But the act of choice is not the same for the two. The British imperial policy (apart from that of the self-governing dominions) has been conducted on a basis of free trade or economic internationalism. A reversion to close imperialism would be for her a retrogression. The United States, on the other hand, has practised a distinctively national economy, and the adoption of a free internationalism would be a great act of faith, or—as some would put it—a leap in the dark. I prefer the former term as indicative of the new truth which is dawning on the world, the conviction that just as an individual can only fully realize his personality in a society of other individuals, that is, a nation, so nations cannot rise to the full stature of nationalism save in a society of nations. For only thus can nationality, either in its economic or its spiritual side, make full use of its special opportunities for the development of a distinctive national character. The supreme challenge is, therefore, not to the continental European nations, not even to Britain, but to America. For her alone the choice has the full quality of moral freedom. For she alone is able to refuse. Other great western nations might seek to stand alone for economic life and for defence. They could not long succeed; they are too deeply implicated in one another's destinies. Even Britain with her vast extra-European territories could not hope to disentangle herself from the affairs of her near neighbors. America could do this, at any rate for some considerable time to come. True she has economic committals in Europe. She has loaned European governments and peoples some ten milliards of money. She is still lending her credit to support the large surplus supplies of foods and other goods she is selling Europe. If this business is to continue, it will implicate her even closer in European affairs. Europe in its present case can hardly be presented as a safe business proposition. If America proceeds along this path, it will be because she looks beyond the immediate risks to the wider future of a safer and more prosperous world. She could now draw out; she could cut the present economic losses of her European loans; she could divert her attention from the European markets to the development of the American continent as the principal area for the disposal of her surplus goods and energies.

It is open to her to take this course. Prudence may seem to dictate it.

The reckless mismanagement of European governments, the wild unsettlement of peoples, the badness of the peace, are,

29

indeed, strong arguments for America cleaving to her old ways.

Europe has no rightful claim upon America, either for the urgent work of economic rescue, or for participation in the permanent project of a society of nations. America not only has the right to refuse; it is probably to her immediate interest to refuse. But, at the risk of misinterpretation, as an officious outsider, I will venture to present an appeal to the wider and deeper interests of Americans. The refusal of America not only shuts the gate of hope for millions of war-broken, famine-ridden people in Central and Eastern Europe, it removes the keystone for the edifice of a society of nations. For effective international coöperation in economic resources and opportunities is the indispensable condition of such a society. No League of Nations can survive its infancy without this economic nourishment. The world's wealth for the world's wants: unless this maxim can in some effective way be realized, no such escape has been made from the pre-war policy of greed and grab as will furnish a reasonable hope for a world redeemed from war—a world clothed and in its right mind.

Is it not the larger and the longer hope and interest of America to live as a great partner in such a society of nations, rather than to live a life of isolated prosperity, perhaps the sole survivor in the collapse of western civilized states? I make this appeal in the language of Edmund Burke, in his great plea for conciliation with America, when he reminded his hearers that "Magnanimity in politics is not seldom the truest wisdom." This, I venture to say, is the true appeal of Europe to America today. Burke's words, I feel, must kindle conviction in every generous heart, for in the last resort it is the desire of the heart and not the calculation of the intellect that governs and should govern human conduct. For morality among nations, as among individuals, implies faith and risk-taking, not recklessness, indeed, but dangerous living, a willingness and a desire to take a hand in the largest game of life and continually to "pluck out of the nettle, danger, safety"; but this safety itself only as a momentary resting-place in the unceasing urge of nations to use their nationality, not for the achievement of some selfish separate perfection, but for the ever advancing realization of national ends within the wider circle of humanity.

* 9 7 8 1 5 2 8 7 1 5 1 5 7 *